The Handbook

A Physician's Insights into Life and Medicine
Core Lesson: Make a Difference

Fray F. Marshall, M.D.

ISBN: 1-4679-2691-4
ISBN-13: 9781467926911

Dedication

This handbook is dedicated to my wife, Lindsay, my children, Wheatley and Brooks, my daughter-in-law, Kami and my grandson Otis Fray. Special thanks need to be given to Jerry Wilson, who supported these efforts in every way, Clintonna Cross, who painstakingly helped revise many versions, and Sadler Poe for all his help in the management of this book.

TABLE OF CONTENTS

Background of books by Fray F. Marshall, M.D.

Marshall FF, Elder JS In: <u>Cryptorchidism and Related Anomalies</u>, Praeger Publishers, New York, NY, 1982.

Marshall FF: editor <u>Urologic Complications</u>. Year Book Publishers, Chicago, IL, 1986; 2nd Ed., Mosby-Year Book Publishers, Chicago, IL, 1990.

Marshall FF: ed. <u>Operative Urology</u>. W.B. Saunders Co., Philadelphia, PA, 1991.

<u>Textbook of Operative Urology</u>. ed. Marshall FF, W.B. Saunders, Philadelphia, Pennsylvania, 2nd Ed. May, 1996.

Issa MM, Marshall FF: Contemporary Diagnosis and Management of Diseases of the Prostate. <u>Handbooks in Health Care Company</u>, Pennsylvania 1st Ed. 2000; 2nd Ed. 2004; 3rd Ed. 2005.

Dr. Marshall has more than 275 articles published in medical journals.

Preface

Donald S. Coffey

Dr. Fray Marshall provides the reader with tremendous wisdom and insight that he has collected as sayings based on his broad experiences in so many facets of life and medicine. Fray Marshall grew up on the playgrounds and in schools in New York City, before continuing his college days in the cradle of democracy in Charlottesville and the University of Virginia. After completing his M.D. there in 1969, he continued three years of surgical residency training at the University of Michigan and then completed a urology residency in Boston at Harvard's Massachusetts General Hospital. He then joined the faculty at the Brady Urological Institute of the Johns Hopkins Hospital in 1975, where he served as the Bernard L. Schwartz Distinguished Professor in Urological Oncology until 1998. During his 23 years at Hopkins, I was most fortunate to be a faculty colleague with him. Senior faculty and young residents at Hopkins still quote Marshall sayings from the "Handbook", even for a decade after he moved to Atlanta in 1998 to accept the Chairmanship of Urology at Emory University.

These sayings originate from Fray's deep interest in all facets of humanity that is always combined with his deep respect and understanding of the individual. His attention to sharing his collected knowledge in simple sayings provides clear beacons to us in focusing meaning on so many practical situations. We all appreciate the sparkle of his spirit that is beamed to us within his wise thoughts. As we travel through life, we all receive inspirations in many forms. One of my own favorites is from the great Albert Schweitzer, who said, "The only ones among you who will be really happy are those who have sought and found how to serve." I have tried to expand this a bit by offering my own version, which is,..."If you only serve yourself, you will not get very good service. If you only make money, you will not make enough."

The nice thing about aging and maturing is that it soon becomes apparent what is important to each of us. This "Handbook" by Fray Marshall may be of help to you on your journey.

Introduction

Make a Difference

The Handbook represents a philosophy that has application to both medicine and life. The Handbook was never actually printed, but became an increasingly utilized reference source in teaching. It is now more formalized with this text and has insights that apply to life experiences. An influential patient approached me with the idea to actually put the material in a written form. I was very fortunate to have my son, Brooks Fray Marshall, review and edit the Handbook. I am indebted to him and his fine recommendations, which have improved the Handbook tremendously.

I owe a great debt to many people who have shaped my career. First, my wife Lindsay has provided constant support, discipline, wisdom and love in my life, and I would not have had a successful career and Handbook without her. She sacrificed much of her career for my career. I am also indebted to my children, Brooks and Wheatley, my daughter-in-law, Kami and my grandson, Otis Fray, who are always bright rays of sunshine for me.

In addition, I have had the good fortune of being trained by superb surgeons and physicians, including Dr. William Fry of Michigan, Dr. Wyland Leadbetter and Dr. Hardy Hendren of the Massachusetts General Hospital. Later, I worked with many incredible individuals at Johns Hopkins Hospital like Dr. Patrick Walsh and Dr. Donald Coffey. They all contributed immensely to my development and indirectly to the Handbook. I want to thank them all.

I may be a surgeon and teacher, but I learn from my students and residents. They are an integral part of the continuing education of their teachers, whether that is in the academic setting or elsewhere. For that reason, this handbook will hopefully appeal to a broad swath of the population. I hope that some of these chapters will allow you to approach life with the backdrop of helping yourself through helping others.

I. LIFE'S LESSONS—GENERAL

"Passion is an important ingredient for success"

Intelligence, personality, money and many factors can be ingredients in achieving success. On the other hand, the spark that lights the fire to foster continued achievement toward a long-term goal is passion. If one is not passionate about work or a project, it is much harder to correct problems or overcome the obstacles that arise in the path to success. Difficult personalities, regulation, lack of money, mistakes and a myriad of features can derail any process. It is only when you add passion to the overall equation that success will be achieved.

Individuals can sometimes find themselves in an occupation that doesn't suit them and there may be few options for other kinds of work that could be more stimulating; however, it is always better to bring passion to one's work. The workplace can be improved by someone who helps others and creates a more favorable environment. In our Department of Urology, we try to have a family orientation. A warm, caring environment increases productivity and fosters better health. Corporations whose passion is to improve the workplace, their products, and the life of their employees are usually more successful.

"Always plan for the worst case scenario"

In the hospital, complex patients frequently have difficult medical and surgical problems that require treatment. It is important to have potential plans A, B, C and D when approaching a difficult treatment or management problem. For example, management issues may change dramatically during an operation. Before complicated surgery, it may be important to arrange access to a blood cell saver and consulting surgeons as well as have three or four treatment plans in mind. It is always best to plan for the worst case scenario. No one wants bad things to happen, but it is possible to anticipate problems and prepare for them.

My grandfather and father were both heavily influenced by the Great Depression of the 1930s. Poor outcomes needed to be anticipated so that they could be successfully managed. My father built a fireplace in the kitchen so that if power were lost in the house, he could not only heat part of the house, but also cook for himself. In fact, he did lose power once during a snow and ice storm and was perfectly at ease by himself cooking sausages and beans over the fire. As I have always told my children, there will always be unanticipated expenses related to a car, condo or child. Plan for them with a rainy day fund. In life and medicine, planning for the worst case scenario is likely to produce a better result.

"Never forget where you came from"

People who come from humble beginnings and make notable achievements in life should always be proud of their origins. I am surprised that there is sometimes an intimidation feature that exists in wealthy "higher" social settings. My father came from Culpeper, VA, but spent most of his working life in New York City. At work and in social settings, he would often remind people of his agrarian roots. His small town roots were always a source of pride, not ridicule. You are what you are and be proud of it. You will never be wrong.

"Satisfaction is derived from meaning and purpose in life"

A significant number of people in the world worry about their next meal. The majority of people are also unhappy with the work that they perform to survive. A smaller, privileged group likes their work and derives much satisfaction from it. Medicine is such a profession because it gives you the opportunity to have meaning and purpose in life and be excited about your work.

Nevertheless, it is not necessary to be a physician to derive meaning and purpose from work. I once knew a janitor in the hospital who was immensely proud of his work. He came up with an idea to put disinfectant in his mop solutions each night when he cleaned hospital floors. This act was fortunately recognized, and ultimately he became a technician in the operating room. He made a difference, just as we all can.

"Many people look but do not see"

Frequently, what needs to be seen is right under our nose, but is not appreciated. I once had a patient who was sent to the emergency room for right lower abdominal pain and probable appendicitis; however, the pain had a specific distribution and raised the possibility of a urinary tract problem. Careful x-ray investigation found an obstructed right kidney, not appendicitis. Fortunately an appendectomy was not performed and the obstructed kidney was drained due to this diligence. Careful observation gave this patient great results.

Powerful art also has the capability of showing us what we might not "see" every day. We may not have recognized the beauty of a leaf with frost on it or a tree in the evening dusk. We have seen thousands of leaves and may have walked by that same tree for years, but we can occasionally witness it in a new light. I once saw Central Park in New York City from an entirely different viewpoint even after looking at it for many years. During a walk home from school across the park, I traveled through a magnificent snow storm and did not glimpse one other person. It was a peaceful setting that seemed to transcend the urban landscape.

We can also learn lessons from the Native Americans, who lived in harmony with their environment. They understood the forces of nature and the lives of the plants and animals all around them. Many an Indian scout saw what was necessary to see because his existence depended on this ability. He only killed as many buffalo as he needed to feed and clothe himself, as opposed to the settlers who did not have this appreciation. The Native American tended to leave the environment as he or she found it because it would serve them well again in the future.

Careful observation can advance medicine, increase appreciation of art, improve the environment, and even help in survival.

"All men are immortal until they are fifty years old"

The aggressive male usually thinks he can conquer most things. This sense of invincibility is especially true for young and healthy males (as most men under 50 seem to view themselves). It is not unusual to see a man in his 40s who thinks he can behave and perform like a man in his 20s or 30s. Professional football players can be tempted to play into their 40s—at least until they get hurt. Many successful boxers will also fight much later in life and injure themselves when their reflexes are slower. These great athletes are considered the best and have led a glamorous, rich life. It is hard to give up the excitement of the lights, money and visibility.

Only after 50 do the realities of aging and life become apparent. Some of these great athletes have not planned a new career and may not view themselves as capable of creating a new career. By looking ahead and recognizing that the athletic talent level is decreasing, they can create a more orderly transition and ensure that their legacy remains intact.

The same is true in medicine. In our urology training program, we try to give our residents the tools for constant learning, so they can take their experience as they age and couple it with new medical information to continue improving urologic care.

It is important to learn and to evolve because there are always new challenges in life that have to be overcome.

"We are divorced from the environment"

The world is experiencing increasing problems from an expanding population, pollution and over consumption. In the United States, most people have not seen an animal slaughtered in order to provide a McDonald's hamburger. The population may not be aware that the insecticides, fertilizers and many other agents used to produce our food end up in the water supply. It is hard to find unpolluted water in most of the planet, and in major cities during much of the year, it is hard to find clean air to breathe. We need to be more concerned about air, water and the environment for future generations.

I had the good fortune of growing up in Manhattan in the winter and in a small log cabin in Virginia in the summer. Both worlds were great, but one came to know nature and the environment when there was no air conditioning or other luxuries that we presently enjoy. Life was still very good in the rural setting given how much nature had to offer. In the log cabin, I slept on a screen porch, listened to the deafening sound of crickets at night, experienced storms blowing across the bed, and ultimately awoke to the sounds of beautiful birds as the sun came up.

To paraphrase John Muir: you can find yourself by losing yourself in the wilderness.

"People isolate themselves because of insecurity"

We all experience interaction with difficult people. When they speak, they may make arbitrary and dogmatic statements and become challenging in the work setting. It has often been my observation, however, that these individuals are very insecure.

Emphasizing an individual's positive rather than negative traits can produce positive results. Individuals respond to compliments in a powerful way.

On the other hand, some behaviors such as bullying can require more direct action. I have taken the dangerous step of addressing a superior about what I considered unacceptable behavior. Results can be unpredictable, but in this case, my life improved significantly thereafter.

Always try positive actions before any negative activity, but remember to stand up for what you believe in.

"Small things can get big in a hurry"

In medicine and life, paying attention to detail is critically important. What may seem like a small detail, such as putting an additional suture in surgical reconstruction, can sometimes make the difference between a complication and an easy recovery. A small medical problem can expand and produce a wide range of potentially disastrous complications.

Similarly, a small, unrecognized social insult or slight may become a major issue in the future. In fact, the insensitive individual may not even perceive that he or she has made a previous negative comment.

In our daily lives, we are absolutely dependent on the individuals we work with. Occasionally, we may have a patient arrive in our clinic that is initially quiet, but then becomes upset and agitated. We are fortunate to have several wonderful medical assistants who are usually able to appreciate and understand the concern of the patient and notify the physician so the problems are addressed promptly and directly. We live in a digital world, but we strive for a personal approach in our clinic to ease patients' concerns and enhance their care. The same scenario occurs daily in the business world. It is much better to deal with someone's concerns promptly before they escalate.

Good relationships with colleagues, patients or customers can keep small things from getting big in a hurry.

"A woman's radar is better than a man's"

In general, women are more likely to be sensitive to their social setting and interpersonal relationships than men, particularly when it comes to subtleties. Perhaps it is how they are trained in our society, but they seem to grasp the nuances of dress, intellect, motivation and overall social behavior more quickly than men.

Along these lines, a mother has an uncanny sense of when inappropriate social behavior will happen or has happened. In fact, my mother could usually tell when all four males in our house were misbehaving in different activities at the same time. She also had no trouble pointing out this behavior. My wife, Lindsay Marshall, has excellent radar. I remember one incident where the entire faculty considered a colleague to be brilliant, outstanding and essentially better than anyone else. In spite of this, Lindsay always had reservations that I could not understand. Ultimately, the individual became a convicted felon, proving her initial reservations to be absolutely correct. As in many families, my mother always had that same instinctive radar that anticipated bad personalities or poor behavior. She was rarely wrong.

By looking through the prisms of my mother and my wife, I have learned to pay close heed to women's opinions.

"Life is more than just your investments"

In medicine, one has the luxury and pleasure of being able to interact with a wide range of people. Many people seem to worry more about their investments and their material well-being than their health. Possibly some are in a state of denial, but the only priceless commodity in life is life.

In extreme circumstances, there is no question that bankruptcy and financial distress can cause great personal and mental harm. A lack of savings and a high lifestyle can result in ruin both financially and spiritually. It is always possible to live more simply and save. When I was first married and starting my career as a urologist, my wife continued to make some of her clothes. We lived in a fourth floor walk-up apartment in Boston, but we had a great life. When we moved to Baltimore and I joined the Johns Hopkins University faculty, we lived in a rental apartment with no washer or dryer and only had one car. Even many years later, I drove a car with a rusted hole in the floorboard and the kids loved looking down at the road. We lived simply, saved and enjoyed life.

As I learned from my grandfather and great-grandfather, investments are a means, not an end.

"Greed and fear of death drive all human activity"

Although there are many complexities written about life and the evolution of life, human motivation for many can be distilled down to two ingredients: greed and fear of death. However, if I talk to a group of younger males, they will almost invariably add sex to this list.

In some ways, this simple statement represents a callous approach to life. I think many may actually refute this dismal analysis through the inspiration of family and by helping others. There are numerous outstanding examples of individuals who have risen above this attitude, including leaders like Gandhi, Martin Luther King, Jr., Abraham Lincoln and many others.

Happiness is more likely to be achieved when fear of death and greed are not dominant.

"The intangibles dictate most major decisions in life"

Important decision making requires a close evaluation of all aspects of the situation. I have often been impressed, however, that intangibles and emotional responses dictate many major decisions in life. For example, you usually select a mate based on how you feel about him or her rather than your analysis of their objective features. Similarly, in an abundant job market, you are likely to select a position as much by its "feel" as by objective criteria.

At the end of my urology training, I was released from my obligation to the Armed Forces. I had no job and a new baby had just arrived. I knew many chiefs of urology departments around the country, but soon met Dr. Patrick Walsh, who had just started as Chairman at Johns Hopkins in Baltimore. At the time, Baltimore was really an aging, rust belt city and the hospital and clinic were very old as well. There were more glamorous departments in other cities, but I liked the chief, the tradition and the overall feel of a future position at Johns Hopkins. I made a great decision to go to Johns Hopkins, but it may have been less obvious at the time to others.

Gut feelings should not be dismissed. It is not unusual for some of these feelings to be more easily understood over time.

"The most impressive people are always the most humble"

Most people can usually tell when someone is bragging or overrating themselves. In general, actions speak for themselves, and there is never any reason to overstate one's accomplishments or views.

During high school, I played quarterback for the school's football team. In one particular game, we were in a very tough contest but were driving close to our opponent's goal line. The players who usually made suggestions for plays were unusually silent, and I wasn't sure what play to call myself. The right halfback was the shyest, quietest person on the entire team, but on this occasion, he said "let me try and take it in." On the next play, he scored a touchdown. Everyone on our football team had a more positive view of this person after that play, but it was mostly due to his understated approach. He demonstrated ability through his actions rather than his words.

We had a brilliant scientist in our laboratory who understood science and people as well as anyone I know. He would often describe his very unassuming beginnings in rural Tennessee. He flunked the fifth grade and had dyslexia, but he ultimately persevered and achieved great success, all the while remaining humble. He became a revered professor in three separate departments, and at one point, director of a cancer center. His influence was pervasive in both science and human interaction. He was able to understand other peoples' viewpoints and almost universally assist them with any problem.

Humbleness nurtures ability.

"There is elegance in simplicity"

The beauty of nature provides a good lesson in simplicity for all of us. Trees and plants often function well because of a simple design. Similarly, animals usually have straightforward designs to allow them to function most efficiently with the least expenditure of energy.

The flight of a bird is more complicated than an airplane, but it is done in a simple, elegant way. We are just beginning to understand the magnificence of a bird in flight. What appears to be a basic wing design allows a bird flying at 40 miles per hour to land on a moving branch in a matter of seconds. There is no machine like that at present, and it would be hard to recreate the pure majesty of this movement.

We can easily have our entire life devoured by television, music, cell phones, texting, computers and children's events, not to mention our jobs. Some of my best ideas for new procedures or experiments occurred when I was just sitting without any distractions.

Simplicity in life provides an element of order.

"It is better to under promise and over deliver;
however, most do the opposite"

When anyone first arrives in a city, would more useful information come from the mayor, the head of the chamber of commerce or the taxi cab driver? I would vote for the taxi cab driver as he or she will likely give you a more realistic assessment of the city and what is closer to reality than a top politician. Unfortunately, we see too many people in high positions who over promise and under deliver. There is a strong tendency in human nature to be grandiose. It would be refreshing to see more of the opposite. Although politicians may not be able to perform in this manner, a credible leader who expects to be in position for a long time is better served by under promising and over delivering.

A member of our Urology Advisory Board, Mr. Chuck Warren, agreed to help the Department raise $2 million for a research chair. "Help" for him meant spearheading the effort that successfully funded the chair. This is a man who said relatively little in the beginning, but his leadership ultimately delivered in spectacular fashion.

In the context of delivering, there is an important distinction between a promise and a goal. Goals should be set high as it is only through high goals that great achievement is accomplished.

Not everyone can deliver like Chuck Warren, but a good leader understands that it's teamwork and hard work rather than lofty promise that produce success.

"Our work is an honest expression of ourselves" (Hodge Kirmin, Elevator Operator, Gallery 291, Alfred Steiglitz's Gallery, 1917)

Hodge Kirmin was an elevator operator for Gallery 291, which was owned by Alfred Steiglitz. This was the first gallery devoted primarily to artistic photography in New York City. Although Mr. Kirmin ran the elevator in the gallery, everyone who visited the space met Mr. Kirmin. He always felt part of the artistic effort and understood intuitively some of the innovative features related to the art. Steiglitz helped identify and promote artists who were relatively unknown at the time in the United States, but subsequently became artists of great renown. These artists included noted photographers such as Steichen and Westin, but also other artists such as Georgia O'Keefe and August Rodin. Mr. Kirmin understood the vision and mission of the gallery and was an important part of it.

In our hospital, we have a wonderful man named Sylvester who runs our information desk. Sylvester tries to help all the patients and visitors who come to the hospital. Many are distressed and upset given their circumstances. He takes excellent care of these people and appreciates the importance of his role in trying to relieve human suffering. He understands the vision and significance of the hospital and is just as important as anyone else who works in it.

"What is the most important ingredient in life?—Time

Ask ten individuals about the important ingredients in life and you'll get ten different answers. Material possessions, money and power are all important, but if one runs out of time, they become meaningless. As we stated in another chapter, investments can become more important than the patient's health; however, accumulation of physical things can and will become meaningless. In my own life, after developing cancer, it became more and more obvious that the principal important aspects of life are family, friends and a positive relationship with them and the environment. My wife, son, daughter, daughter-in-law and grandson are a constant source of enjoyment. They continue to inspire me.

"Humor helps us survive"

Everyone experiences dark hours during the course of life and at the end of life. Most understand the dark side of experiences, but some levity allows us to continue in a somewhat happier world. We might as well try to enjoy our existence while we are here rather than lament it.

We have all seen examples of individuals who inject humor into very negative situations and this humor allows us to cope much more effectively. The entire nation of Ireland had hundreds of difficult years as a result of domination by the British, famines and extensive migration. Somehow in spite of all these difficulties, the Irish frequently tend to have a great sense of humor that has allowed them to survive in a better way.

Similarly, for me and my patients, a little humor can be a strong, positive force.

"It is selfish to be altruistic"

Although this statement may appear to be initially contradictory or para-doxical, it is not. Man is a social animal and does better when there are favorable contacts with fellow man. It is family and friends that often sustain an individual as we age and develop an increasing number of problems. Without their sup-port, life would be much shorter and less fulfilling. We all derive immense intangible benefit from a positive social environment. Everyone is more likely to be helpful to you if you have been helpful to them in the past. In addition, helping others also gives the individual a sense of worth and meaning. I have received personal satisfaction almost daily by trying to benefit patients in my care. It is therefore in the individual's interest to behave positively, even if you are not deriving immediate benefit from helping someone else.

"What is the best predictor of future performance?— Past performance"

In our department, we hire new resident doctors each year. Fortunately, they are intelligent, arrive with glowing letters of recommendation and have scored well on all the entrance tests. We often ask ourselves how you predict the future performance of these individuals. Some score better on the entrance tests, but have not always had a stable, consistent record of success. An individual who may have inferior test scores, but has exhibited consistency during his or her previous career, is often more stable and a better choice than someone who is very intelligent with a mixed prior record. Occasionally, the individual who has overcome one or two adverse events in his or her life may also be an attractive candidate. Someone who has overcome adversity in the past is likely to overcome adversity in the future. When evaluating a person, it is always best to step back and look at the entire package.

"Great players can make coaches look good.
Great coaches can make great teams."

There are many brilliant coaches in football. On the other hand, if there is someone who can run, pass or excel in some capacity, then a coach may look better because of this player and not because of himself. For that reason, it is always important to applaud all the players on your team.

I have seen coaches strike players or harshly criticize them. Negative reinforcement may work partially in the short term, but these coaches can destroy self-esteem and ultimately change the life course of an individual. Positive reinforcement does much better over the long term. It may be possible to take a mediocre player one year, and with continued work, make him or her a starter the following year.

With a football team, as with any organization, it's not just the abilities of the individual players that count, it's how those individuals play (or work) together.

A great player (or employee) can make a coach (or boss) appear great, but a great coach (or boss) can mold a great team.

"What is in print is not always valid"

The written word has become more suspect now that there is the internet where one can choose between email, blogging, social media and many other modes of unedited expression. Even if the written word appears in a medical journal or some erudite publication, it does not necessarily mean that it is true or valid.

There are many processes in medicine that provide for checks and balances. We have weekly conferences that review patient cases so that the original management opinion may be altered if appropriate. We also have a journal club where we review articles on medicine. Once these publications are carefully reviewed, points of debate can be generated in essentially all papers.

Both inside and outside the field of medicine, it is always better to make an assessment of source and material before accepting the accuracy and validity of the conclusions expressed.

"People make it happen, not rules"

There can be no question that rules are necessary to govern the way we act. Government often thinks that making a law will provide the intended result, but sometimes regulation can become burdensome, inappropriate and highly inefficient. Worse still, people learn to comply with the letter of the law in order to avoid its intent. Simply put, if rules supplant human judgment, we are all the poorer. If people believe in what is good and appropriate, they should make it happen and not be totally governed by inappropriate rules.

There are numerous rules that govern medicine. Currently, regulatory agencies are trying to restrict the work hours of residents-in-training. At present, the maximum is eighty hours per week, but there are proposals to limit it to sixty hours or less. These manpower regulations will dramatically change the practice of medicine and create significant financial costs. If one interprets these rules rigidly, a resident doctor-in-training taking care of a sick patient could conceivably go home because he or she has fulfilled the hourly maximum for that week. Clearly, we would expect this doctor to make sure that the medical care of this patient is appropriately managed before he or she leaves work regardless of the number of hours clocked.

Rules are not always the silver bullet.

"The gardens of Kyoto, Japan!"

During a visit to Japan, I experienced the splendor of the gardens of Kyoto. These gardens have provided a greater understanding of the environment and life. Many were constructed more than five hundred years ago. Their beauty is hard to describe, as the blend of water, rocks, flowers, plants, and temples are all combined in a magical fashion. I have told many people that I think the beauty of the gardens of Kyoto reflect art and nature. They can be summarized as "the perfection of the imperfect." I believe that the best gardens are the most contrived, natural environments you will ever see. In other words, there is a sensibility that is transmitted to the observer through nature, art and the environment.

We all should appreciate the beauty of nature whether it is the oceans, mountains, prairies, woods, garden or even a local park. We are all dependent on our environment. The gardens of Kyoto reinforced my appreciation of nature and our need to preserve it.

"Urban living—it may be difficult to have roots when you only have cement under your feet"

My family comes from a rural Virginia heritage. The Marshall family came from small towns in Virginia, and I spent summers in a log cabin with no hot water. In the winter, however, I lived in Manhattan and enjoyed all the benefits of a large city with a great education, art and a vibrant urban life. City life has appeal, but I still cherish my familiarity with red clay, trees, mountains and the overall Virginia environment. We are dependent on water, grass, trees and all that comes from the earth. If the earth is entirely covered by concrete and asphalt, we would be divorced from all that ultimately sustains us. This understanding is important for the survival of the world.

"It is not whether you get knocked down, but whether you get up——Vince Lombardi"

During life, everyone gets knocked down. It is possible to lose family, loved ones, jobs, money, homes or almost anything in life. In some ways, a loss can then allow the individual to reflect on the event. In these difficult times, if there is a large loss of money, can life be lived in a simpler and less expensive way? It may be possible that a less extravagant life may actually be a more pleasant and productive life. By learning from difficult experiences, an individual can put his or her life in perspective and ultimately improve life by making a few changes in attitude. For example, if one enjoys good health, then many of the material losses may not really be that important because there is always the possibility of continuing your life with good health.

When we are knocked down, it is critical that we get up and continue to play. I once received a bad grade in organic chemistry, which is a pre-requisite for medical school. The odds against my admission to medical school seemed to grow exponentially, but I redoubled my efforts and success followed.

It is important to persevere and follow what you believe because there is a good chance that you will be rewarded.

II. LIFE LESSONS FROM MEDICINE

"Saturday night hands"

The Handbook was never actually printed, but its verbal heritage continued to grow over the years with significant additions from residents. Some actually thought it was a book, but it was not formalized until late in my career.

One of the early sayings that caught other physicians' attention was "Saturday night hands." Its origin stemmed from an observation that a resident surgeon-in-training can occasionally be aggressive and a little rougher than necessary in the operating room. When I observed that behavior, I would often remind them that it is important to have Saturday night hands during any surgery. Most medical students and residents-in-training understood this phrase, but occasionally someone would ask about its meaning. It encourages hands that are soft and delicate, but with plenty of purpose.

"Never seen a prep too wide"

An early idea in my training involved never seeing a prep that was too wide. This quote really came from an orthopedic experience where wide preps were very important. Operations start with preparation (prep) of the skin with an antiseptic solution. A new person in the operating room may prep a small area of skin for an operation when a wider area is more appropriate for sterile technique. For example, in orthopedics, an entire leg may need to be prepped for extensive surgery because the operative reconstruction can be more extensive than originally contemplated. Along those lines, I have seen roof leaks that have been repaired in the same location many times. In this situation, a wider investigation and repair with more extensive reconstruction of flashing corrected the problem.

A broad view of the problem may be helpful in many circumstances.

"Where does wisdom come from?—Bad experience"

Medical students and residents frequently create long lists of qualities that result in wisdom. These include hard work, intelligence, passion, etc. I often tell them I believe that wisdom most frequently comes from bad experience, which can include everything from complicated operations to difficult patients.

If an operation is contemplated to fix a problem with the kidney, prior experience in training or in practice can help us realize that we cannot plan the operation by focusing solely on the diseased kidney. A particular kidney operation may seem very simple, but at the time of operation, there may be many adhesions and problems from previous abdominal surgery. It only takes one difficult operation to recognize that previous abdominal surgery can sometimes make additional surgery much more complex. A negative experience in my career always made me think of alternatives in management going forward.

Although this example is in medicine, there are many examples in other areas of life. For instance, a salesman may tell us that their product and workmanship is the best, but after the purchase we come to realize that their work is really poor and more costly. Next time, we will know to listen less and do more investigative work.

Bad experience can improve our judgment and aid the physician, the businessman or the consumer in the future.

"Before you point the finger, be sure you point it at yourself first"

In a discussion, it is rare that the speaker is ever at fault for anything. It is almost always someone else. In the operating room, it is rarely the surgeon's fault as well. An operating team is essential for a successful procedure; therefore, a surgeon's personality should never be so large that it negatively impacts the operation.

We must remember that sometimes an observation that may not be the same as ours can actually be correct. While constructive criticism can always be offered if there is a variance of opinion, most speakers should take a critical look at themselves before offering their advice. We have a weekly conference where complications and medical issues are discussed throughout the Department of Urology. It is easy to offer criticism of other physicians, but all the physicians ultimately have patients who have had problems. Each doctor can benefit by analyzing their own performance in the context of their team and by listening to constructive comments. I have had a few patients where placement of an extra drainage tube would have prevented a fluid collection and abscess that had to be drained. If I had analyzed my own performance in this context, the excess fluid could have potentially been avoided. This process can be very humbling, but remains important in the evolution of the surgeon and the individual.

"You can't operate on what you can't see"

Clear visualization and understanding of a problem, whether it is in surgery or in life, is critical before one can operate or fix the problem. If there is a major problem with surgery, it is often because visualization is poor. For example, if a surgeon is in trouble and needs assistance, it is frequently helpful in open surgery to make a larger incision to allow one to see the operative field more clearly. The operation is generally improved when one focuses initially on exposure rather than immediate technical features of completing the procedure.

We need to operate on many problems in life. It is not unusual to be embroiled in a specific emotional argument that doesn't present an easy resolution. If one steps back and takes a broader view, it becomes clear that the emotional turmoil may be related to something else like a job loss, death in the family or other seemingly unrelated issues. A broad view can be helpful for a specific or narrow problem.

You can only fix what you can see and understand clearly.

"Our horizons are dictated by the extra urologic experience"

It is important that a urologist's education is broad. The field is constantly evolving, and as a result, one needs the intellectual tools and overall capability of adjusting to the changes that will certainly occur. As an example, we have always stressed that urology residents have exposure to general surgery training because they need wide training to be able to understand how to take care of problems in the chest, abdomen and elsewhere. After all, they will be operating in all of those areas.

Although we live in an era of hyper specialization, we still need to understand the entire, complex patient, and not just a segment of the patient. Many jobs in and out of medicine can be defined by an increasingly narrow skill set. It is important to have a broad base of experience to allow for flexibility in a changing world. I wrote in one of my books ten or fifteen years ago that I was not originally trained to perform 90% of my present operations. On the other hand, I had the principles from previous training to learn how to do these new procedures to benefit my patients.

"In research, the unexpected finding may be the most informative"

In research, investigations often provide expected answers. So much so that unexpected results may shock the investigator. But it is precisely the unexpected finding that may be the most informative. Of course, the investigator needs to determine if this unexpected finding is real. If so, then a new vision can be created. Examples of this unexpected phenomenon range from stomach ulcers to obstructed vessels.

When I started in general surgery, stomach ulcers were always thought to result from an acid problem. Many operations were performed to reduce the acid supply of the stomach. The entire treatment was focused on giving oral antacids or surgically reducing gastric acidity. More recently, however, it has been demonstrated that an infection can cause these ulcers in a process that is entirely different than was originally perceived.

Until recently in heart surgery, arteries were reconstructed with the patients' veins or their own arteries, but it became apparent that it was possible to place a little plastic tube in some of the coronary arteries and avoid a major operation. This whole process actually started several decades ago. Dr. Grunzig at Emory decided that it might be possible to pass a wire into an obstructed vessel, balloon dilate it, and manipulate it without replacing the entire vessel itself. In my career, I designed a retractor system for a radical prostatectomy operation in order to improve visualization. It functioned so well that it rapidly became clear that I did not need a second surgical assistant, which provided a more efficient staffing model. Pay attention to the unexpected. It may be informative.

"I like nipples, just not the urological ones"

In an extensive urinary tract reconstruction, nipple-like structures can be created surgically from bowel to actually direct the flow of urine. In urology, often the bowel is doubled over on itself or intussuscepted to create an anti-reflux ("anti-backwash") component for urine, which is the nipple structure. But if intussusception occurs clinically, it can create bowel obstruction and patients must have surgery to reduce the intussuception. Therefore, the bowel does not like to be placed in this position, and I have never been attracted to its use as an anti-reflux mechanism in the construction of new bladders with bowel despite the fact that it was a commonly used operation.

Just because a technique becomes popular does not always mean that it is the best and most appropriate. We are all sometimes influenced by popularity rather than a superior course of action.

"Perception is reality"

Physicians can mistakenly think they know exactly the status of the patient, the diagnosis and treatment. On the other hand, if the patient thinks that he or she will do poorly, I pay a lot of attention to these remarks even when I think the patient should do well. A patient's perception of him or herself and their disease should always be taken into consideration because his or her perception is reality for them. Sometimes the doctor's explanations may or may not change that perception. I know of a tragic case of a doctor who had a bad cancer in his leg, and the tumor was removed. He later felt another mass in the same leg and assumed that he had recurrent cancer. He then committed suicide, but the post-mortem examination revealed no cancer. While this is an extreme example, maintaining hope for a patient adds to longevity.

Just like in marriage or business, communication remains critical and can help avoid negative outcomes.

"Re-approximate the normal anatomy"

Normal anatomy provides a guideline for future reconstructions, but many new operations include the use of foreign material or create situations that represent a marked departure from normal anatomical circumstances. The normal anatomy of the body provides a wonderful template for any reconstructive surgery. For example, operations can include cardiac reconstruction or genitourinary reconstructions, such as the formations of new bladders out of bowel. In general, an operation is more likely to be successful over a longer period of time if the surgeon tries to re-approximate the normal anatomical structures as much as possible rather than relying on artificial material or new gimmicks that may have the potential to create as many problems as they solve. Foreign material such as surgical mesh can become infected or erode.

If it is possible, use normal anatomy as a possible template for future reconstructions, preferably with tissue rather than foreign material.

"We don't grab what we sew; we show what we sew"

The basic techniques of surgery should include good visualization and delicate, precise tissue handling. I learned early in my training that surgery is not a rough or mechanical exercise.

Surgeons sometimes have a tendency to grab tissue and sew it immediately. Whenever tissue is handled aggressively, the micro-circulation is negatively impacted. Therefore, it is better to hold adjacent tissue aside to allow the surgeon to visualize the tissue to be reconstructed. A needle is then placed through the tissue under reconstruction and it receives minimal trauma and maintenance of its micro-circulation. This technique improves healing as well.

Just like handling tissue in an operation, it is as important to be delicate and respectful of personal interactions. Brusqueness and indifference in social settings are no less damaging than they are in the operating room.

"What gets us into trouble? It's not what we don't know; it's what we do know that ain't so!"

This statement is a paraphrase from Will Rogers and was actually a favorite of my father, Dr. Victor F. Marshall. We all carry biases for extended periods of time, but it is sometimes surprising that the most important part of a learning experience is to understand that the "new truth" is actually the opposite of what we thought the old truth represented.

A hundred years ago, no one thought surgery could be performed on the heart. A new heart valve can now be placed in the heart, even when the heart is temporarily stopped and the patient is put on a heart-lung machine. Moreover, heart valves can be inserted through the blood vessels rather than subjecting the patient to open heart surgery. This minimally invasive heart surgery represents an exciting change for the better through the new truth.

There is very little in life that is static. We need to be careful when we believe we have permanent knowledge of a specific subject because it can easily change.

"Make one cut for a surgical incision"

Surgeons frequently utilize the cautery to burn their way through the tissue. This technique can injure normal tissue. Other surgeons use a knife and make many cuts through the tissue. One single knife incision is often better because it devitalizes less tissue and there is less tissue damage than with the use of cautery. There are times in surgery when there is significant scarring, and utilization of the knife is critical to continue with surgery. Sharp dissection is sometimes viewed as more difficult and dangerous, but it may be the best way to perform certain operations and achieve an adequate exposure. Other techniques may be equally, if not more dangerous.

As with a surgical incision, a single straight or right path in life is not always the easiest. It may raise the most resistance. Focus is important as *easy* does not necessarily mean *best*.

"In modern molecular medicine, diagnosis precedes therapy"

As research evolves in the characterization of the molecular and genetic features of diseases like cancer, it is increasingly possible to identify certain kinds of cancer and help predict their response rate to different kinds of treatments. A diagnostic test will likely occur before a treatment is achieved for a specific tumor on a molecular basis.

As the normal human and cancer genomes are dissected, identifiable markers will be discovered to predict the presence and aggressiveness of different cancers. Specific malignant, molecular pathways can be blocked later to provide effective treatment with less probability of toxicity.

Knowledge of the normal human genome and understanding of many of the variations that occur in cancer do not always lead to immediate diagnosis and treatment. There is so much genetic variability in cancer that it is sometimes very difficult to identify predictable markers or expected therapy. Once the markers are identified with more precision, however, more effective therapy is likely to occur. There are many researchers working tirelessly to give us new tools for the diagnosis and treatment of cancer. These researchers often do not receive high salaries, but are just as dedicated as the physicians. As medicine evolves, they deserve continued support. It was a privilege for me to have worked with many of them.

"What is the biggest thing in the operating room?— The surgeon's ego"

Confidence is important for a surgeon to be able to effectively complete an operation; however, sometimes an ego is so large that it becomes an impediment to a successful outcome. In my training, I was exposed to a few arrogant, sometimes abusive surgeons. If this behavior became extreme, control was occasionally lost in the performance of the operation. It is important to remember that not only in surgery, but also in most facets of life, management is more effective by a team rather than an isolated individual.

Another corollary to this issue is the difference between arrogance and confidence. An arrogant person is less likely to listen to another individual or other points of view. Confidence can be helpful and arrogance can be detrimental. A confident, capable surgeon is likely to lead an effective team and produce good results for patients.

"God and nature allow us to get away with a lot"

There can be a tendency to be sloppy, delayed or inappropriate in actions and words when the surgeon is tired and the procedure is long. It is just as important to be sharp and vigilant at the end of the procedure as the beginning. I've been involved in operations that took 10-12 hours. At the end of these long operations, the reconstructive process was often the most demanding and intense part of the procedure. Despite the fatigue, attention to detail and precision is critical for a good result.

It is absolutely amazing what the human body can do to heal itself in many occasions. On the other hand, it is important not to depend on an overall healing process (nature) or God to provide the best result. It is the surgeon's efforts that still provide the best result.

"With molecular treatment of cancer, there is more specificity and less toxicity"

Most chemotherapy agents tend to target rapidly dividing cells. These agents may kill cancer, but they may also disrupt normal, rapidly dividing cells in the body, which results in hair loss, GI symptoms, etc. Both as a cancer patient and practicing physician, I have not always been attracted to standard chemotherapy because of the unpleasant side effects. Fifteen years ago, I had the good fortune of working with a fabulous research group at Johns Hopkins that utilized gene therapy as a novel form of chemotherapy for prostate and kidney cancer. I was attracted to this approach because of its potential higher level of specificity with the theoretical lower incidence of toxicity. We are now just beginning to see some of these new forms of treatment.

Early identification of molecular pathways in the diagnosis of cancer can allow later development of agents that block these specific pathways. Under this approach, toxicity can be reduced while improving quality of life. Toxicity is a major risk factor in chemotherapy, and it needs to be addressed just like treatment of the disease.

"Utilize the least number of maneuvers to accomplish a task"

Often a task may be performed in a long and laborious way. For surgeons, it is important to perform the operation with the least number of maneuvers to accomplish a task. A shorter operation done efficiently is typically less traumatic than a longer one. Brevity does not mean fast movement, but efficiency of action.

Efficiency should be prescribed for clinical research as well as surgery. In clinical research, there always needs to be a targeted goal, and tests can be ordered to measure progress toward that goal. But I have been involved with clinical research where regulatory agencies and oversight committees have become so cumbersome that when the actual study was finally approved, it had already been closed because patients had been accruing at other institutions.

Mixing brevity and efficiency with a well-reasoned approach will usually produce a good result.

"You can learn from anyone"

A physician resident-in-training receives instruction continually from nurses, technicians and other hospital staff. It is often those individuals who provide some of the best education for someone new on the job.

I once worked with a fabulous male nurse named Rudy in the burn unit during general surgery training. Many of these burn patients were very sick and had difficult management problems. Rudy was an African American nurse who put himself through school to obtain his registered nurse degree. He had worked in the burn unit for a long time and had a tremendous ability to guide young interns and residents through a maze of difficult patient management problems. The patient and intern always had a knowledgeable advocate in Rudy, and he helped to save the lives of many patients.

Sometimes a physician may not pay enough attention to the entire medical group involved in the continuum of care. Nurses, medical assistants and even janitors make major contributions to the care of the patient. Similarly, we can all learn lessons from individuals at all rungs of the professional and social ladder.

In Closing

The Handbook was a flexible tool to initially help medical students and residents-in-training; however, it encompasses not only medically oriented sayings but also philosophical suggestions for a better life.

The dominant theme is that anyone can make a difference. It is important to think of and help other people, because you, the individual, will benefit. This benefit can occur at all levels. Younger individuals can make a difference for senior people around them, but the older personality requires a level of respect given the perspective developed with age.

After I discuss the qualities that we desire in applicants for our department, I always add a second statement about the evolution of the department. These applicants are being hired not only to help others, but also to continue the education of the chairman. Learning is always a two way street as younger brain circuitry is less fixed than an older brain, so creativity is often more likely to evolve from a younger brain.

I remain hopeful that the young and older mind will both converge and set their sights on making a difference. That would be my ultimate prescription.

Personal Reflections

Personal Reflections

Personal Reflections

Made in the USA
Charleston, SC
19 March 2012